Love,
Mom

Mirabelle Grace

On the day our eyes first met

I experienced a love that was new,

Like the beautiful warmth of a summer sunset

And as fresh as a morning dew.

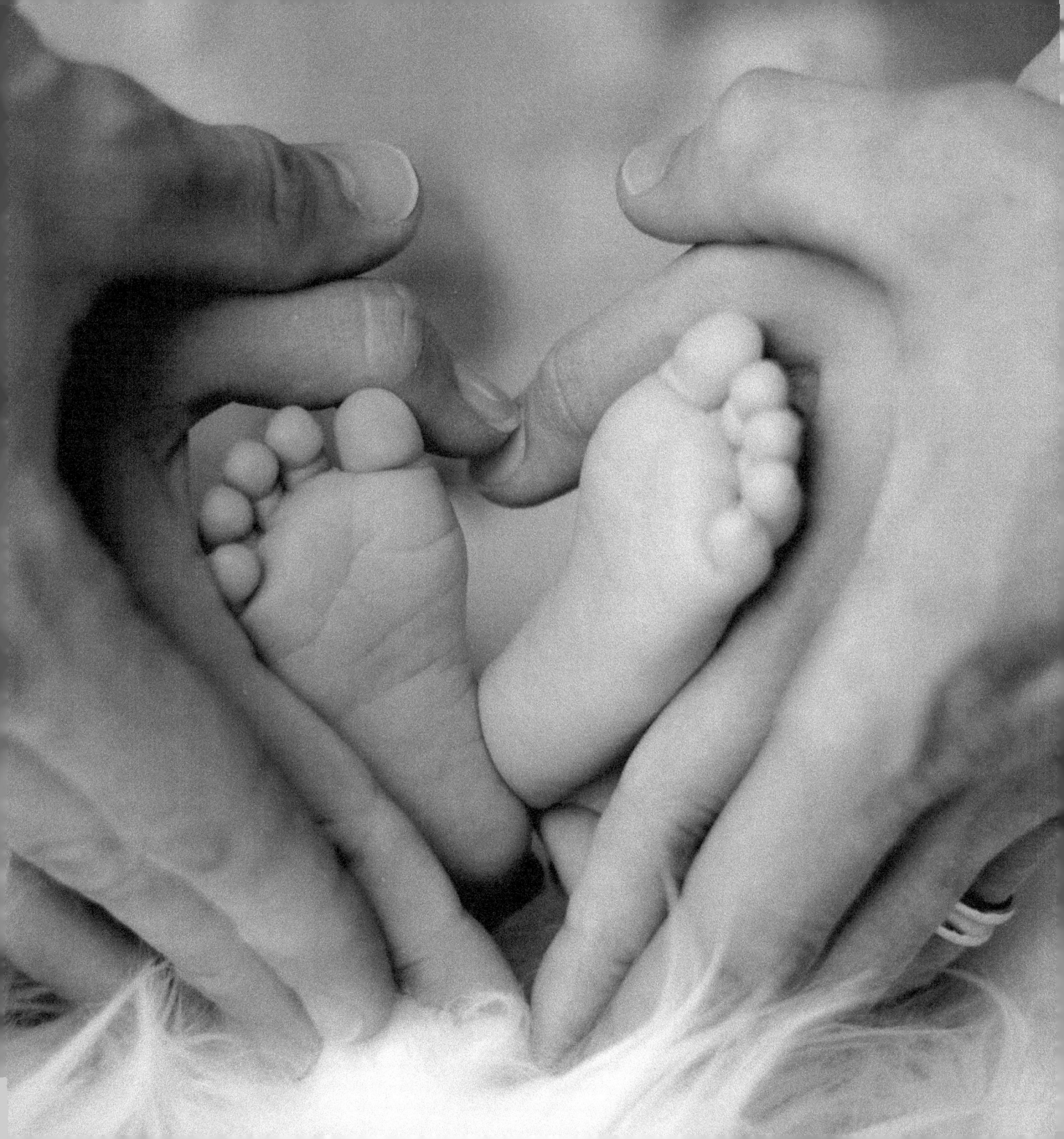

Now, as you grow each passing day,

I'm reminded of what I once knew:

I didn't give you the gift of life.

Life gave me the gift of you.

You'll always be my pride and joy,

My wonderful, spirit-filled child.

So, as I recall all the things you have done,

Every day may not be good,

but seek to do good every day.

Be brave. Be bold. Be beautiful.

I'll encourage you all the way.

Remember to smile more and worry less;

Persistently follow your dreams

Be the very best YOU, you can ever become,

And take challenges to the extremes!

Life will bring thrills, valleys and hills,

They'll be times you may have to backtrack.

You're never alone, I hope I have shown,

When life gives you lemons and rainy days,
Learn how to make sweet lemonade.
Stay positive, humble, and never forget:
Let nothing make you afraid!

Keep moving forward with your face to the sun

And you'll never see the shadows.

Laugh, love, live, celebrate and have fun.

There are only so many tomorrows!

Believe in yourself as much as I believe in you.

Be the glue when it all falls apart.

And though you may fail, overall, you'll prevail,

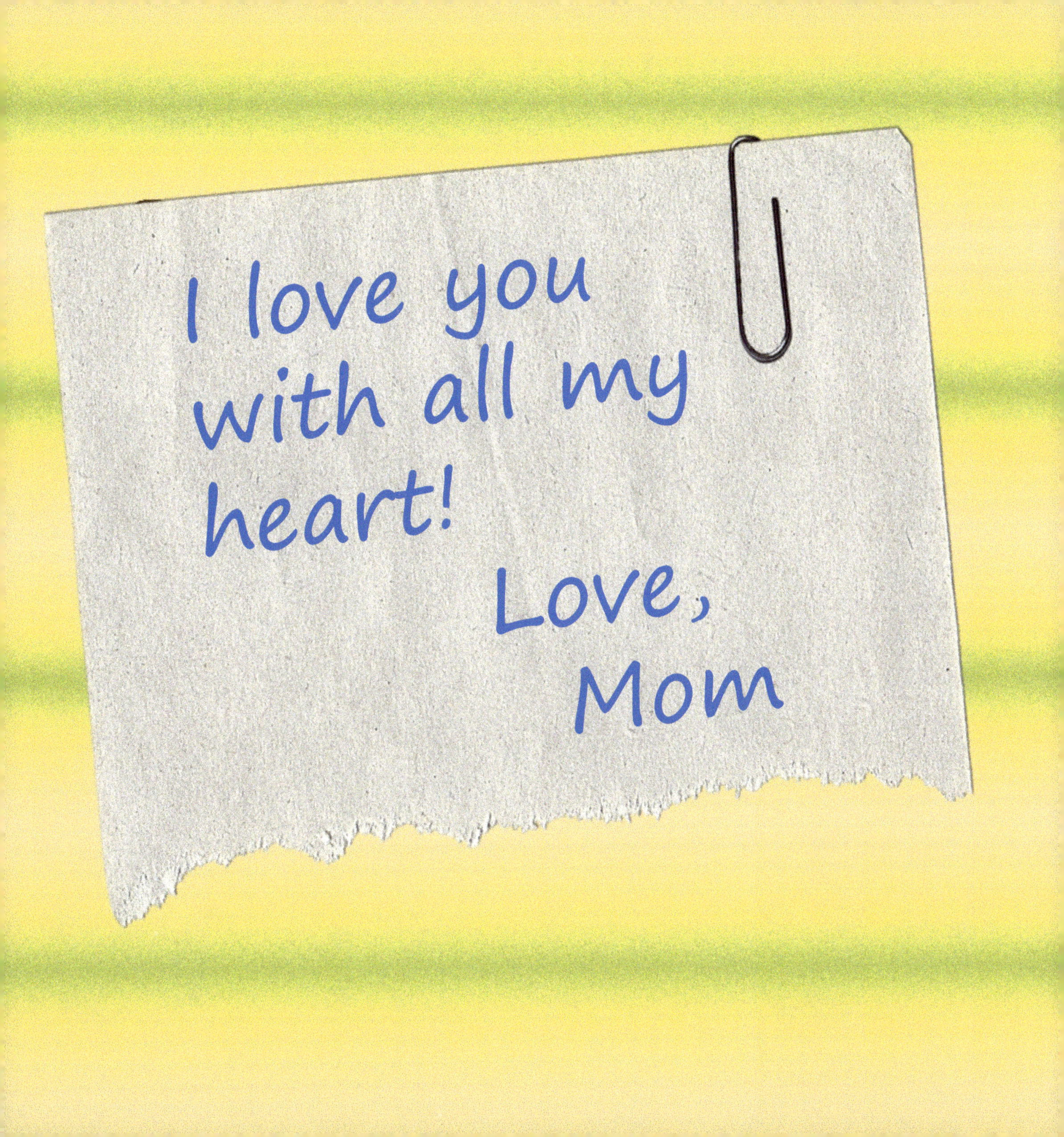
I love you
with all my
heart!
Love,
Mom

Everyday that you are not with me

I wonder what you are doing.

No matter how old, or how far you go,

My thoughts, and my love, are pursuing.

As the days turn gray and fade away

You'll always be my sunshine;

I can't promise to be here the rest of your life,

but I'll love you for the rest of mine.

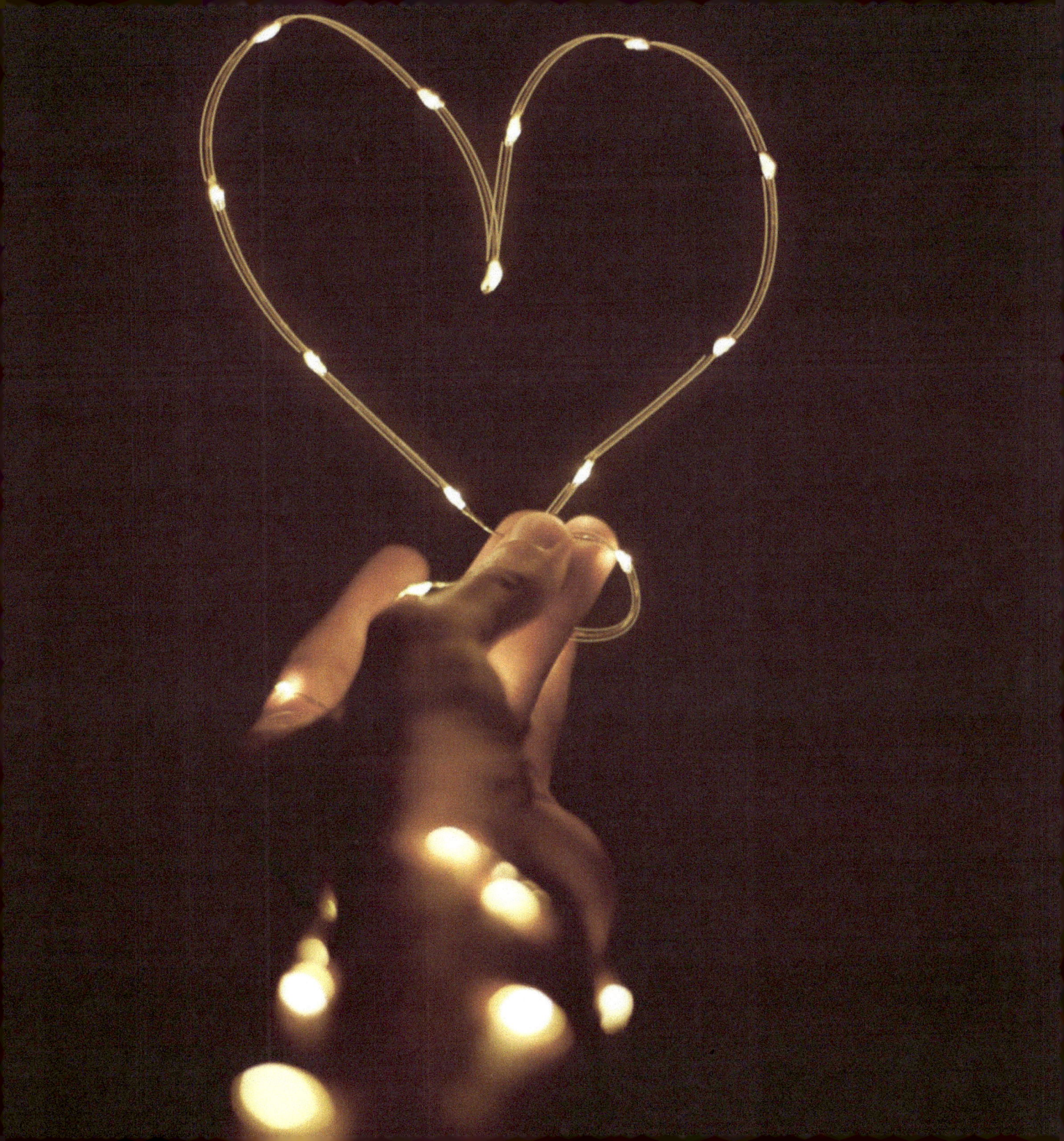

My love will surround you wherever you go

And embrace you, whatever you do.

Alone or with friends, until this life ends,

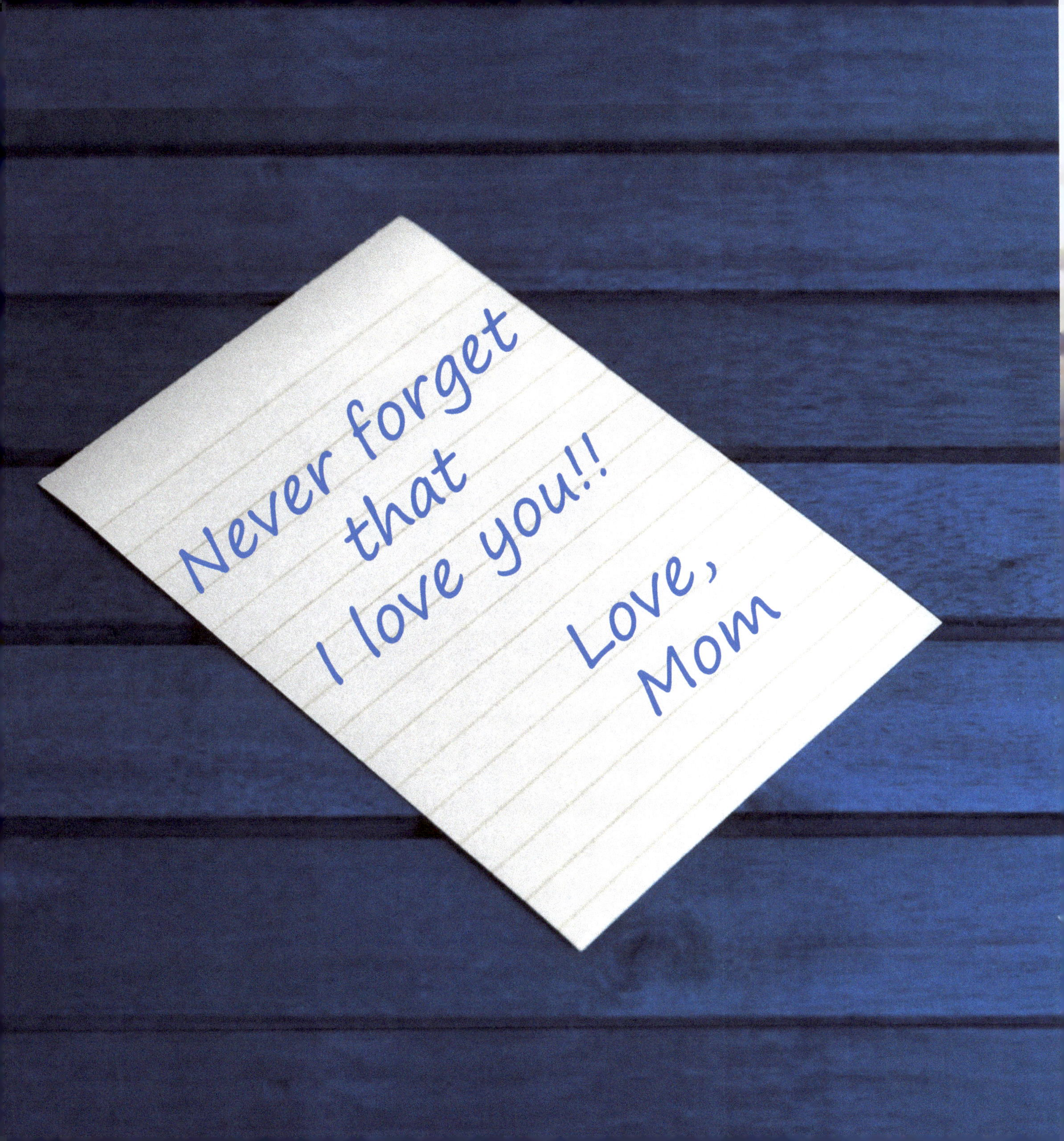
Never forget
that
I love you!!
Love,
Mom